WONDERS OF THE WORLD

ANTARCTICA

Jean F. Blashfield

Technical Consultant

Dr. Donald B. Siniff
Department of Ecology, Evolution, and Behavior
University of Minnesota, St. Paul

RSVP
RAINTREE
STECK-VAUGHN
P U B L I S H E R S
The Steck-Vaughn Company

Austin, Texas

A production of B&B Publishing, Inc.

Editor – Virginia Lowe
Photo Editor – Margie Benson
Computer Specialist – Katy O'Shea
Interior Design – Scott Davis

Raintree Steck-Vaughn Publishing Staff

Project Editor – Helene Resky
Project Manager – Joyce Spicer

LIBRARY OF CONGRESS CATALOGING-IN-PUBLICATION DATA

Blashfield, Jean F.
   Antarctica / Jean F. Blashfield.
      p.   cm. — (Wonders of the world)
   Includes bibliographical references (p.) and index.
   ISBN 0–8114–6366–4
      1. Antarctica—Juvenile literature.   [1. Antarctica.   2. Natural history—Antarctica.]
I. Title.   II. Series
G863.B58   1995
919.8'9 — dc20

94-40911
CIP   AC

Cover photo	Title page photo	Table of Contents page photo
King penguins, Salisbury Plain, South Georgia Island	**Antarctic landscape of snow, ice, and sky**	**The Ross Ice Shelf is a massive ice field permanently attached to the continent.**

PHOTO SOURCES

Cover Photo: David G. Houser © 1992

Courtesy of Blakeslee Group: 15 right
© Capitol Systems Group: 11 left, 12, 16, 21, 22, 25, 26, 30 left, 52 left, 53
© Capitol Systems Group/Chris Finley: 19
© Capitol Systems Group/Brad Guttilla: 52 right
© Capitol Systems Group/Ann Hawthorne: 17 both, 20, 31, 50 right, 51 top, 52 left
© Capitol Systems Group/Russ Hinne: 9 right, 29 right, 32 left
© Capitol Systems Group/Dirk Meenan: 56
© Capitol Systems Group/NSFA: 40 right, 49 left
© Capitol Systems Group/NSF: 37 right
© Capitol Systems Group/Julie Palais: 51 right
© Capitol Systems Group/Phil Sadler: 49 right
© Capitol Systems Group/P.R. Taylor: 27 left, 32 right
© Capitol Systems Group/Trombecky: 9 left

Courtesy of Dava Still Media Depository: 47 right
Greenpeace photo by Liz Carr: 13, 59
Greenpeace photo by Keith-Nels Swenson: 48 top
© William R. Hammer: 24 bottom
Courtesy of Captain Glenn Howell: 15 left
NASA: 54 both
National Park Service photo by Robert Belous: 18 right
National Park Service photo by M. Woodbridge Williams: 29 left
© Dick Olenschlager: 1, 3, 14, 24 left, 27 right, 37 top, 40 left, 41, 42 right, 45 right, 57 left
© Sylvia Stevens 1993: 4, 8, 11 right, 18 left, 28, 30 right, 33, 35, 38 both, 39 right, 42 left, 45 top, 50 left, 55 both, 57 right, 58 left, 60
Courtesy of the U.S. Naval Academy Museum: 15 right
© Chuck Webb/The Antarctica Project: 47 left

Printed and bound in the United States of America.
1 2 3 4 5 6 7 8 9   VH   99 98 97 96 95 94

Table of Contents

Chapter One

This Place of Extremes

Until a few centuries ago, the world's human population did not know that there was anything but a frigid sea at the bottom of the globe. They certainly didn't dream that there was an ice-covered continent located at the South Pole.

Polynesians had approached but never explored Antarctica. Then, in the late 1400s, geographers proposed that there must be a vast southern continent to balance the weight of the big northern ones—Europe, Asia, and North America. On their maps, they placed a huge continent they called Terra Australis, meaning "Southern Land."

Gradually, seagoing explorers began to look for this land, but the furious, cold seas kept them from going far enough south. Constant cloud cover hid the continent. A fruitless three-year search convinced Captain James Cook that though there might not be the huge continent imagined by the philosophers and mapmakers, there must be some kind of land producing all the floating ice he saw. However, he also became certain that if there were indeed such a continent, "the world will derive no benefit from it."

Finally, in 1820, explorers from three different nations went beyond the floating ice, called pack ice, and sighted the continent. It was another 20 years before it was generally accepted that the land they saw was, in fact, a continent.

Virtually every sea captain who first ventured into the area cared only about the pursuit of fur-bearing animals. All their energy was expended on the hunt, the great storms, and the cold. It was another 50 years before humans actually started investigating the continent on foot. Then, within a few years, great heroes began to write their names in the history of Antarctica.

The explorers sought the location of the South Pole. Roald Amundsen, the first explorer to reach the South Pole, had to locate it with compasses and star sightings—and then just hope that his reckoning was right.

The Earth rotates on an imaginary line called

"I have been more deeply lonely in Antarctica, a place I love as much as any on earth, than anywhere else. Maybe it is sharpened, like every sense in this place of extremes, by the violence of the wind and the poignant pale lightness of the calm days' blue silence."

— Michael Parfit in
National Geographic

An emperor penguin strolls past the base of an iceberg in Antarctica.

its axis. The South Pole is the point in the Southern Hemisphere where the axis ends. It is the farthest south that it is possible to go. Today, the ceremonial location of the South Pole is indicated by a silver globe mounted on a red-and-white-striped barber pole. It is located at an elevation of 9,200 feet (2,800 m), all of which is ice. The exact location of the pole is marked with a copper pipe.

Just What Is Antarctica?

Above all, Antarctica is ice. But beyond that, Antarctica, or the Antarctic, can be defined in a variety of ways.

First, Antarctica is the continent on which the South Pole is located. About 1.5 times the size of the United States, Antarctica is the Earth's fifth largest continent. It has an area of 5.4 million square miles (14 million sq km), or about 10 percent of the Earth's land surface. However, unlike all other continents, only a little actual land is visible because 98 percent of the continent is concealed by ice. During the winter, enough additional ice freezes around the edge of the continent to add an apparent 8 million square miles (21 million sq km) of ice to the continent, as much area as another whole Antarctica. But then in summer, the ice melts and disappears again.

Antarctica is much larger than the United States. The black outline of Antarctica has been placed over the United States, Mexico, and Canada on the map above to show the size comparison.

Second, the Antarctic is the area within the Antarctic Circle, located at 66° 33′ S. That latitude marks the beginning of the southern "land of the midnight sun," where the sun never sets during the polar summer. The land within the Antarctic Circle includes most of the continent and a number of islands. Only the merest fringe of East Antarctica and the tip of the Antarctic Peninsula extend north of the Antarctic Circle.

By a third definition, the Antarctic includes the region within the Antarctic Convergence. The Convergence is the boundary formed by cold Antarctic water flowing northward, meeting warmer

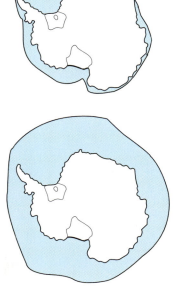

The top map shows the boundaries of Antarctica's ice in the summer. The bottom map shows the boundaries of the ice during winter.

Early morning fog shrouds the largest island inside the Antarctic Convergence, South Georgia.

water flowing southward. It is a roughly circular band about 25 miles (40 km) wide. At its most northerly point, it reaches about 47° S, which is farther north than Tierra del Fuego, the southern tip of South America. At its most southerly point, on the Ross Sea side, the Convergence sinks to past 61° S. The largest island within the Convergence is South Georgia.

All the water within the Convergence is part of the South Pacific, South Atlantic, and South Indian oceans. It covers a total area of about 13.9 million square miles (36 million sq km).

The Antarctic Treaty, which preserves the south polar region for scientific study by all nations, provides a fourth definition. It protects the entire area south of 60° S.

Coldest, Windiest, Driest . . .

Antarctica is a place of extremes. In addition to being the most isolated place on Earth, it can be the coldest, the windiest, and the driest. It is also both the highest and the lowest continent.

The temperature can drop below −120°F (−85°C). Ice is everywhere, averaging 7,070 feet (2,155 m) deep. Antarctica's average temperature is

35°F (20°C) colder than the Arctic's average temperature. It is nearly always below freezing everywhere on the continent, as well as on the sea up to about 60° S. Antarctica's temperature varies between –76°F (–60°C) on the top of the dome-shaped ice sheet to 14°F (–10°C) along the coasts.

The south polar region is known for its incredible winds. In more temperate climates, wind direction is fairly predictable. It blows from areas of high air pressure to areas of low pressure. But Antarctica has katabatic winds, which means "downward-flowing." These gravity-driven winds start on the central plateau of East Antarctica and roar downward toward the coast, speeding up along the way, until they may reach 200 miles (354 km) per hour. And the direction they come from depends on the twists and curves of the land they cross while flowing downward. Early explorers marveled at the strength of the wind. They had to lean so far forward to stay "up" that they were walking almost horizontal to the ground.

A survival school student at Scott Base on Ross Island learns to "navigate" across the seemingly endless ice of Antarctica.

Heading out over the sea, the katabatic winds hit the warmer air over the ocean, causing violent storms. From the earliest days of sailing in the water surrounding Antarctica, sailors recognized the special quality of these winds by calling the latitudes such names as the Screaming Sixties, the Furious Fifties, and the Roaring Forties.

The land of ice and snow is also a desert, the driest on Earth. It gets less precipitation each year than the Sahara does! How can that be? What snowfall there is—less than 2 inches (5 cm) per year—doesn't melt or soak into the ground. It just lies there, year after year, decade after decade, gradually compressed by the weight of the newer snowfall above it, until it turns to glacial ice.

Asia has Earth's highest mountain peaks. The Andes in South America have more mountains over 10,000 feet (3,040 m) high than any other continent. Yet Antarctica can rightfully claim to be the highest continent on Earth. The central plateau of

Huge glaciers such as Beardmore Glacier (below) move toward the outer fringes of Antarctica.

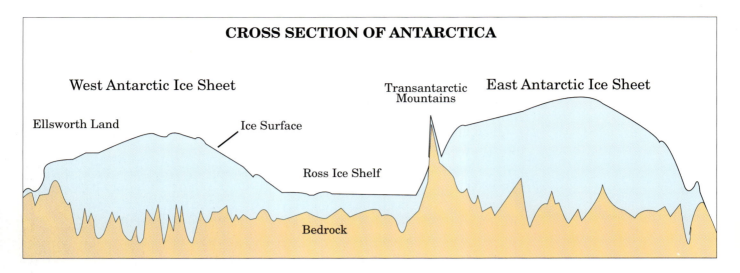

CROSS SECTION OF ANTARCTICA

West Antarctic Ice Sheet

Ellsworth Land

Ice Surface

Transantarctic Mountains

East Antarctic Ice Sheet

Ross Ice Shelf

Bedrock

Most of Antarctica's elevation comes from huge ice sheets. The East Antarctic ice sheet is much larger than the West Antarctic ice sheet.

East Antarctica has an average elevation of 2.5 miles (4 km). However, the single highest mountain is not in East Antarctica. It is the Vinson Massif, which reaches an altitude of 16,860 feet (5,140 m) in West Antarctica.

Most of the elevation comes from the ice sheet. The bedrock underlying the ice is actually lower than the bedrock of any other continent. Most of it is below sea level, held there by the weight of the ice.

Comparing Arctic and Antarctic

If all these extremes exist at the South Pole, don't they also exist at the North Pole? After all, the word *Antarctic* means "opposite of the Arctic." They are both in the "high latitudes"—regions where the degrees of latitude are in the 70s and 80s. The opposite ends of the planet, however, are really quite different.

The Arctic consists of an ice-covered sea surrounded by land, while the Antarctic is ice-covered land surrounded by sea. Their respective geographies create very different climatic conditions.

The coldest temperature recorded in Antarctica occurred on July 21, 1983. The temperature dropped to –128.6°F (–89.8°C) at a Russian scientific station. The coldest temperature in the Arctic was recorded at –93°F (–70°C) in Russia. One reason for this difference is that the sun's rays are reflected back out into space more readily from the white ice that covers Antarctica than from the Arctic, which has, at least in summer, large areas that are not ice-covered. The Arctic atmosphere is able to retain more heat.

The Arctic is often defined as the region within an imaginary line connecting places that have an average summer temperature of 50°F (10°C). The Antarctic doesn't even have places that reach such a high temperature.

Approximately matching the Arctic's 50° temperature line is the tree line. North of it, trees don't usually grow, but bushes and flowers thrive—close to a thousand species of flowers bloom in the Arctic. The continent of Antarctica, by contrast, has no bushes and only two types of flowering plants.

Animals such as fur seals live on the warmer coastal areas of Antarctica.

The Arctic, which includes parts of several continents, has a wealth of animal life. Caribou and polar bears are the best known. Antarctica, however, has no land mammals. The largest animal that actually lives on the continent is an insect called a midge—only 0.5 inches (1.3 cm) long! Larger sea animals congregate on the icy fringes of the continent.

One thing the Arctic and Antarctic have in common is ice—and plenty of it—though, again, the south has much more than the north. Because ice plays such an important role in the lives of the Inuit and other native Arctic people, they have numerous words for different kinds of ice.

Ice that occurs in flat, round clusters is called pancake ice.

In Antarctica, too, an entire ice vocabulary has developed. In the oceans surrounding Antarctica, the water begins to freeze at 28.8°F (−1.8°C). It has an oily appearance, due to a type of ice crystal called frazil ice. This ice gathers into large, flat, rounded clusters that look like pancakes— hence its name—pancake ice. Gradually, as the temperature drops, the pancakes stick to each other, forming ice floes. There's also brash ice, bergy bits, grease ice, ice caps, ice sheets, and more. Only a long-time resident understands—or even needs to know— the differences among the many kinds of ice. People who return to Antarctica again and again refer to it as simply "The Ice."

Another thing the two polar regions have in common is that they provide the outlet for the planet's heat. The sun's rays strike most directly at the equator. Then the heat moves toward the poles, where it

AN ICE GLOSSARY

bergy bit – a chunk of floating ice less than 33 feet (10 m) across that originated in a glacier

brash ice – floating ice fragments less than 6 feet (2 m) across; remains of an iceberg

fast ice – ice attached to shore that is less than 6 feet (2 m) high

floe – an ice chunk not derived from a glacier

frazil ice – needles or small plates of ice suspended in seawater

grease ice – frazil ice joined together into a thick top layer on the water

ice cake – floating ice less than 33 feet (10 m) across

ice cap – dome-shaped glacier, smaller than an ice sheet

but up to 20,000 square miles (50,000 sq km) in area

ice floe – floating ice more than 33 feet (10 m) across

ice rind – grease ice frozen together into a brittle sheet

ice sheet – a huge glaciated area covering more than 20,000 square miles (50,000 sq km)

ice shelf – ice attached to shore that is more than 6 feet (2 m) high

iceberg – a large chunk broken off a glacier that is more than 16 feet (5 m) high

pack ice – floating ice not attached to shore that may be on the open sea or very close to land

pancake ice – flat, roundish plates of ice, usually with a raised rim

escapes back out into space as if from an exhaust pipe. This flow of air to the poles makes the atmosphere of the whole planet circulate. However, the katabatic winds of the Antarctic suck in more warm air from the equatorial regions than does the calmer air of the Arctic. It has been truly said that the Antarctic drives the weather engines of the entire planet.

A Beauty to Preserve

American explorer Richard E. Byrd said of Little America, his base in Antarctica, "There was great beauty here, in the way that things which are also terrible can be beautiful." Antarctica is not just a place of science and statistics. It is a realm of great beauty, often made so by the strange things that sunlight does in the very dry and dust-free atmosphere. Ice crystals in the air send light skittering in strange directions, creating halos around the sun, the moon, and even on the ice. Fogbows challenge the charm of rainbows, and incredible sunsets mark the end of the Antarctic summer.

Living things add to the fascination. Friendly seals with childlike faces, charming penguins that congregate in thousands, graceful birds that appear to fly forever on delicate wings—all of them live in a place that seems so opposed to life.

The most recent living things to visit Antarctica are the tourists who come to see what so few people before them have seen. Hundreds come every year, with their numbers rising all the time. It will be up to the tourists and the scientists to determine whether the south polar region remains hospitable to all living things.

The seaward edge of an ice shelf consists of vertical cliffs.

Wright Valley, one of Antarctica's dry valleys, is not covered with a permanent ice cap. Its stark beauty cannot be matched anywhere.

Chapter Two

Exploring the Icy Continent

Tradition holds that a Pacific islander first saw Antarctica more than a thousand years ago. Recorded exploration began when geographers of the late 1400s proposed the existence of a southern land, Terra Australis. Hopeful Europeans convinced themselves that it must be a tropical paradise with a great deal of natural wealth and, of course, many people to whom European products could be sold or bartered. In 1738, Bouvet de Lozier, a French sea captain, caught glimpses of a large, ice-covered island at approximately 55° S, where it had been assumed there was no land at all.

The British chose Captain James Cook to search for Terra Australis. Cook left England on the flagship *Resolution* in July 1772, accompanied by a second ship, *Adventure*. His journey took him south of the Antarctic Circle three times. He found that lands that others had claimed to be Terra Australis were, in fact, fairly small islands. He sailed farther than 71° S, and in the process came upon South Georgia and the South Sandwich islands.

Stopped by the ice, Cook was glad to have a legitimate reason for turning back northward. He had seen enough to report that there was no continent. But he did wonder if there might be some kind of land farther south, because the ocean birds he saw needed a place to breed. He wrote in his log: "I can be bold enough to say that no man will ever venture farther than I have done; and the lands which may lie to the South will never be explored."

He was wrong. After Cook returned home and reported what he had seen, more than 200 sealing and whaling ships descended on the area. They succeeded in almost eliminating fur seals within a few

Today's Antarctic explorers use all kinds of boats and land vehicles to travel in Antarctica. The picture shows a boat called a Zodiac.

"We proceeded to the greatest and most solemn act of the whole journey—the planting of our flag. Pride and affection shone in the five pairs of eyes that gazed upon the flag, as it unfurled itself with a sharp crack, and waved over the Pole. . . . Five weather-beaten, frostbitten fists they were that grasped the pole, raised the waving flag in the air, and planted it as the first at the geographical South Pole."

— Roald Amundsen describing reaching the South Pole in 1911

short decades. In 1820, a fur seal pelt brought about $5, and the men on one vessel could kill as many as 50,000 animals in one hunting season—earning the equivalent of several million dollars today.

It was these whalers and sealers who first explored Antarctica and began to map the edges of the continent. However, because many of them did not wish to advertise their best hunting areas, they didn't publish their findings. Instead, knowledge spread by word of mouth, wherever sea captains got together and chatted about where they had been and what they had seen.

Fabian von Bellingshausen, a Russian naval officer, circumnavigated the Antarctic from 1819 to 1821. He deliberately headed for the areas that Captain Cook had not entered because he had no desire to compete with his exploring hero. Unlike Cook, Bellingshausen sighted two islands within the Antarctic Circle. He named them Peter I and Alexander I. He may have seen the continent, too, though he never claimed to have done so.

Charles Wilkes, the leader of the 1839-40 United States Exploring Expedition, sailed the *Vincennes* around the coast of Antarctica for 1,500 miles (2,400 km). He reached the conclusion that under all that ice there had to be land—the seventh continent of the planet Earth. He was an extremely harsh commander, however, and was later court-martialed by the U.S. Navy. The British saw his achievements differently—the Royal Geographical Society gave him a gold medal!

U.S. Navy officer Charles Wilkes (right), leader of an expedition to Antarctica, anchored his ship, the *Vincennes,* in Disappointment Bay (below). Wilkes Land is named after him.

The first really big expedition to Antarctica was led by Frenchman Jules Sebastien César Dumont d'Urville. His journey lasted more than three years. In 1840 he claimed part of the continent for France and called it Adélie Land, after his wife. He brought back enough scientific notes to fill 32 published volumes. And he returned to France with an incredible collection of natural history specimens.

James Clark Ross, an experienced Arctic explorer, was sent by the British Admiralty to investigate the magnetic measurements of the South Pole. In 1841, with two ships, the *Erebus* and the *Terror* (names he gave to two active Antarctic volcanoes), he sailed as near as he could to the South magnetic pole. He had hoped to be the first to reach the South magnetic pole because he had already been to the North magnetic pole.

Earth has an iron core that makes the planet like a magnet with a north pole and a south pole. The magnetism is what makes a compass needle point to the North magnetic pole. Unlike the geographic North Pole and South Pole, the magnetic pole moves. Ross had found the North magnetic pole in the ocean, but at the time he went to Antarctica, the South magnetic pole was located inland—a long way from the geographic South Pole—and he could not reach it. In the process of trying, however, Ross discovered the Transantarctic Mountains and the ice shelf now called the Ross Ice Shelf.

James Clark Ross named Mt. Erebus, an active volcano, after one of his ships.

Edging toward the Pole

British explorer Robert Falcon Scott, a 32-year-old naval officer, led the National Antarctic Expedition of 1901-04, also called the Discovery Expedition after his ship. It was the first expedition planned to explore inland from the ocean. The group's first problem came when the ship was frozen into the ice of McMurdo Sound for the sunless winter of 1902.

Ice surrounds Ross Island in McMurdo Sound. Shackleton's ship was frozen in the ice in this same area during the winter of 1902.

As the spring set in and the sun rose higher in the sky, the men began to make short journeys away from the coast by sled, carrying supplies to be left at various depots along the proposed route to the South Pole. On November 2, Scott, Ernest Shackleton, and zoologist Edward Wilson headed toward the pole. However, they were caught in blizzards, and mile after struggling mile, the sled dogs died. Hunger beset both the men and the remaining dogs. They were blinded by snow glare and developed scurvy, a disease caused by lack of vitamin C, which affected their breathing. When the men reached 82°17′ S on December 30, 1902, they knew they must return to the ship. They barely made it back alive.

The Antarctic summer had not been warm enough to release the ship from the ice, so the *Discovery* and her crew spent another dark winter in McMurdo Sound. The long months gave the party time to recuperate so that they could explore again in the spring. The *Discovery* was finally released from its icy prison when relief ships arrived in February.

Shackleton returned home to develop his own plans for polar exploration. However, he was never able to collect enough money for the project. When he returned to Antarctica in 1908 as leader of his own expedition, it was aboard a run-down sealing ship called the *Nimrod*. He made a base at Cape Royds, where 15 men spent the winter in a hut that measured

Shackleton and his men spent the winter of 1908–09 in a small hut at Cape Royds.

only 33 by 19 feet (10 by 5.8 m). In the spring, Shackleton and several others crossed the Beardmore Glacier and, on January 9, 1909, reached 88° 27′ S, within 112 miles (180 km) of the South Pole. Again, hunger was a problem, and the men had to eat their ponies in order to survive. They returned to their hut, ill and starving. However, members of this expedition were the first to climb Mount Erebus and the first to reach the South magnetic pole.

In 1922, Shackleton died on South Georgia Island. His grave site, located on the island, is pictured below.

To the Pole!

Norwegian explorer Roald Amundsen had been the mate aboard the *Belgica,* the ship used in 1898 on a Belgian expedition led by Adrien de Gerlache. Trapped by ice, the men and their ship became the first to spend the winter in Antarctica. The *Belgica* drifted for 13 months while all the men went hungry, and several went mad. Amundsen, however, remained intrigued by polar exploration and prepared to conquer the North Pole. In late 1909, he learned that Robert E. Peary had reached the North Pole first and that Scott was on his way to the South Pole. Amundsen secretly shifted his ambitions to Antarctica, beginning a race that would become one of the most famous—and tragic—in history.

Amundsen anchored his ship, the *Fram,* in the Bay of Whales, 60 miles (97 km) closer to the pole than Scott's location in McMurdo Sound. He and his men built a hut on the ice, and then, in a series of journeys, Amundsen, his men, and many dogs created a series of depots that would hold supplies for the journey to the South Pole. Unlike Scott, who preferred to count on his men to pull supplies across the ice, Amundsen believed in using sled dogs. However, he regarded the dogs as expendable and shot the weakest dogs for food when they were no longer useful. Amundsen also clothed his men in Inuit—or Eskimo—clothing, which Scott scorned.

Amundsen's men wore Eskimo clothing similar to that worn by the Inuit (Eskimo) seal hunters in the picture.

On October 11, 1911, Amundsen, his men, and almost 100 dogs set out for the South Pole. They traveled about 20 miles (32 km) a day and soon passed their last depot. The final days of the journey were an uphill struggle, in the teeth of blizzard after blizzard.

Unlike Scott, Amundsen believed in using sled dogs. Today, dogs are rarely used, however.

As they crossed the high plateau toward the South Pole, they determined their altitude by daily checking the time it took for water to boil. (The higher the altitude, the longer water takes to boil.) They also used dead reckoning—calculating how far they had gone in what direction—to determine their position, but they had to make actual sun sightings with a measuring device called a sextant to prove that they had indeed reached the South Pole. If the blizzards continued and there was no sun, they would not be able to prove they had reached the South Pole. The sun—"shining in all its glory"—appeared on December 14, 1911. Amazingly, their sextant result exactly matched their dead reckoning calculations. They were there!

Because their instruments were not accurate enough to give the exact location of the South Pole, they made a circle 25 miles (40 km) in diameter that enclosed the actual pole. They spent several days trying to determine the pole's location with more accuracy—and making sure they had reached it. Before leaving, Amundsen wrote a short letter to Scott, which he left in a small tent they abandoned at the South Pole along with a Norwegian flag.

Too Late

Robert F. Scott believed that men, motorized sleds, and ponies were the only way to travel in Antarctica. He regarded dogs as too "risky" and "uncertain," and rejected the idea of killing the weakest dogs to feed the strongest. He regarded "man-hauling" as the only safe way to travel.

Scott and his group, sailing on the *Terra Nova*, reached Cape Evans on Ross Island in January 1911. The men soon discovered the inadequacy of ponies in the Antarctic, but it was too late to switch to dogs.

On November 1, 1911, Scott and his party of 15 men left their camp on the Ross Ice Shelf. The motorized sleds broke down, the ponies couldn't walk well on ice, and the men were exhausted from having to pull their own sleds. But that didn't keep Scott from moving ahead with a party of four volunteers. The ponies were shot, and the remaining men and dogs went back to the base camp.

The five struggling men reached the South Pole on January 17, 1912, only to find Amundsen's Norwegian flag flying there. "Great God! this is an awful place and terrible enough for us to have laboured to it without the reward of priority," Scott recorded in his journal.

Scott's hut and skeletal animal remains at Cape Evans are grim reminders of his sad fate.

Their return journey was plagued by blinding blizzards, hunger, and illness. February passed, and the days moved on into March. Still they failed to find their next supply depot. One by one, the men died. Scott kept a detailed log of all events, including his own imminent death.

On March 29, he wrote, "We shall stick it out to the end, but we are getting weaker, of course, and the end cannot be far. It seems a pity, but I do not think I can write more." He signed the entry, but then added one line: "For God's sake look after our people." Months later, the hero's body and his logbook were found in the ice. He had died 11 miles (17.6 km) from his supply depot.

It would be another 44 years after Scott before another human stood at the South Pole. Then it was U.S. Rear Admiral George Dufek who landed

The first women to go to the South Pole were five scientists and a journalist—Lois Jones, Kay Lindsay, Eileen McSaveney, Terry Lee Tickhill, Pam Young, and journalist Jean Pearson—who flew on November 12, 1969, from McMurdo Sound to the South Pole. So that there would be no arguments about who was the first woman at the South Pole, they descended the ramp of their cargo plane arm in arm and all jumped onto the ice at the same time.

at the South Pole in a DC-3. Dufek's visit on October 31, 1956, officially opened United States participation in the International Geophysical Year. The first people after Scott to arrive at the South Pole on foot were members of the International Trans-Antarctic Expedition in 1989.

The Following Years

Other nations were eyeing the Antarctic, too. At approximately the same time as the race to the South Pole, a German group led by Wilhelm Filchner tried to determine whether the Ross Sea and the Weddell Sea are connected. In 1912, the hut they built on the edge of an ice shelf was carried away when the shelf broke. Then their ship, the *Deutschland,* was locked in ice for the better part of a year. They explored new areas but failed in their original objective. Also in 1912, the Japanese turned a too-late attempt to reach the South Pole into a scientific exploration of King Edward VII Peninsula.

Australian geologist Douglas Mawson, who had accompanied Shackleton's *Nimrod* expedition, introduced radio to the Antarctic in 1911. He also started aviation in the Antarctic, though his sled-equipped airplane could do no more than pull sleds of supplies across the ice.

After Amundsen reached the South Pole, explorer Ernest Shackleton set out to achieve a different record—the first crossing of Antarctica from ocean to ocean. His 1914 journey was called the British Imperial Trans-Antarctica Expedition. It failed to cross the continent but lived out another heroic story.

Shackleton let his ship, *Endurance,* get trapped by pack ice. After ten months, the crew jumped onto

The Amundsen-Scott station is located at the geographic South Pole. Americans have been here since 1956, when the station was named in honor of explorers Roald Amundsen and Robert Scott. The station was rebuilt in 1975, with a geodesic dome and steel archways.

a nearby ice floe. They then used their whaleboats to reach Elephant Island. While a group of six men crossed 800 miles (1,287 km) of open water in one whaleboat to get help, the rest survived for 105 days with the remaining whaleboats upturned for shelter.

The complete crossing of the Antarctic continent was not accomplished until 1956, when the British Commonwealth Trans-Antarctic Expedition, led by Vivian E. Fuchs, accomplished the deed. Mount Everest conqueror Edmund Hillary of New Zealand provided assistance by preparing a chain of supply depots and joining Fuchs at the South Pole for the second half of the journey. Fuchs and his team traveled 2,158 miles (3,477 km) in snowmobiles, pulling sleds of equipment.

Australian adventurer Hubert Wilkins made the first flight in Antarctica in 1928. The following year, on November 28, 1929, American naval officer and navigator Richard E. Byrd and pilot Bernt Balchen flew over the South Pole. Byrd observed that there wasn't really a lot to see because the South Pole lies "in the center of a limitless plain. One gets there and that is about all there is for the telling."

The geography of Antarctica had to be pieced together bit by bit, as explorers, whalers, and airmen recorded what they saw. Many of them left their names on the places they discovered. Others have disappeared from history. Since the era of exploration, the polar continent has become the realm of scientists. However, the great whiteness that is Antarctica still holds many secrets.

American naval officer Richard E. Byrd flew over the South Pole in 1929.

GLOBAL COOPERATION

The International Trans-Antarctic Expedition, led by Will Steger of the United States and Jean-Louis Étienne of France, was a party of six men and numerous dogs. They crossed Antarctica from the tip of the Antarctic Peninsula to the coast of Wilkes Land. They became the first people to cross the entire continent on foot.

Steger and Étienne had, by the most extraordinary chance, met at the North Pole. Steger had arrived there as part of a dogsled team that traveled hundreds of miles for 56 days, carrying everything they needed. Étienne had skied there alone. Other members of the international team they put together included Victor Boyarsky, a scientist from the Soviet Union, Qin Dahe, a glaciologist from China, Keizo Funatsu, a dog trainer from Japan, and Geoff Somers, a dog trainer, navigator, and former guide with the British Antarctic Survey.

The group set out on July 27, 1989. For the first time in history, the world watched as TV, newspapers, and magazines reported the progress of the expedition. They reached the South Pole on December 11. They then set off across the vast ice sheet covering East Antarctica, the first people ever to cross this inhospitable and inaccessible region on foot. On March 3, 1990, 220 days after starting and having traveled a distance of 3,714 miles (6,019 km), they were welcomed into the Soviet base at Mirnyy.

Chapter Three

Land of Fire and Ice

The ice: "It's all you notice; it pervades your life—even your dreams," said engineer David Waterhouse in an interview for *Ad Astra* magazine in 1992. Though most photographs and most tales focus on the ice, there is much more to Antarctica.

The Making of a Continent

The continent we call Antarctica has not always been at the cold bottom of the Earth. Instead, it once lay near the equator at the heart of the giant landmass geologists call Pangaea. This "mother of continents" consisted of a number of sections, or plates, that floated on the hot, molten rock deep inside the Earth. Over millions of years, the landmass moved, taking on the different characteristics of the climate in which it was situated.

As Pangaea drifted, the various sections began to separate. First it broke into two major continents. Laurasia, the northern section, eventually evolved into North America and Eurasia. The southern part, known as Gondwanaland, became Africa, South America, India, Australia, and Antarctica, plus other bits and pieces. The final separation came about 60 million years ago, when Australia moved away from Antarctica.

This theory of drifting continents was proposed by geologists on the basis of major rock and mountain formations, landmass shapes, and by matching up the edges of continental shelves like a giant jigsaw puzzle. For example, the rocks of East Antarctica match those in Australia and even North America. The mountains of West Antarctica are really a continuation of the Andes in South America.

The supercontinent of Gondwanaland began to break apart over 180 million years ago, and the separated continents drifted to their present position.

"An Antarctic blizzard at night...is more than just wind: it is a solid wall of snow moving at gale force, pounding like surf. The whole malevolent rush is concentrated upon you as upon a personal enemy."

— Richard E. Byrd, in *Alone,* describing the winter of 1934

23

A Changing World

Antarctica wasn't just a mass of rock waiting to be covered by ice. As it moved around the Earth, life evolved there as it did elsewhere. Dinosaurs roamed the continent and giant marine reptiles swam in its waters. The pouched mammals called marsupials probably originated in Antarctica. They survived only in Australia, along with the opossums in South and North America. Even when the continent was edging toward the South Pole, the climate was such that cool temperate forests grew on it. Fossilized leaves, wood, and pollen have been found to support this theory.

When Antarctica broke away from the rest of Pangaea, it probably had a moderate climate, but gradually it cooled. Glaciation—the building of glaciers—may have started about 38 million years ago. The ice buildup could not have occurred until Antarctica severed its final connection to South America and became isolated from other landmasses. When that happened, the water-circulation and cold-air patterns that surround Antarctica developed.

Perhaps 20 million years ago, there was enough ice buildup for icebergs to begin breaking off, though the main ice sheet on East Antarctica did not build up until about 14 million years ago. Another seven million years passed before West Antarctica was also covered by an ice sheet.

Massive icebergs break off from the huge Antarctic ice sheet, floating and eroding as they age in the water.

FOSSILS IN A FROZEN WORLD

The bones of a formerly unknown carnivorous dinosaur were found in 1991 in the Transantarctic Mountains where the geologist in the photograph is excavating fossils. The new dinosaur was an allosaurus-type reptile that stood about 26 feet (8 m) tall. Between 195 million and 135 million years ago Antarctica was probably located about 20° north of where it is now. The climate there would have been warm enough for the hardy beast.

Among the fossils found in Antarctica was the tip of a bird beak. This was no ordinary bird. The curved tip was just the prying end of a huge 12-inch- (30-cm-) long beak belonging to a 7-foot- (2.1-m-) tall flightless bird often referred to as the terror bird. It probably lived in Antarctica (and, in fact, may have evolved there) when the continent was attached to South America and had a much milder climate. Dr. Judd Case of St. Mary's College in California describes the terror bird's killing method: "What we imagine is that the bird knocked its prey down, stood on it with one foot, and reached down with the beak, ripping out hunks of flesh." The terror bird (whose Latin name means "tearing thief") vanished between one million and three million years ago. Its only living descendant is the 2-foot- (60-cm-) tall carima of South America.

The Continent

The main part of the continent of Antarctica is the large, almost circular area called East Antarctica, Greater Antarctica, or Gondwanaland. Between the two sections, and bordering the whole of one side of East Antarctica, are the Transantarctic Mountains. Opposite the mountains, an edge of the continent projects beyond the Antarctic Circle. In East Antarctica, the mountains reach an altitude of 13,100 feet (4,000 m).

Attached to the center of the mountainous side of East Antarctica is the much smaller region called West Antarctica. Strung out from West Antarctica toward South America, looking somewhat like a long trunk on a small elephant, is the Antarctic Peninsula. A smaller mountain range, called the Ellsworth Range, lies in West Antarctica.

Nestled within a slight curve at the southern end of the Transantarctic Mountains is the South Pole. The South magnetic pole, which marks the straight-south direction of a compass, has moved over the past several centuries, from the Ross Sea across the mountains of Victoria Land, and out into the Indian Ocean.

The ice sheet covering the continent is higher along the edges than in the center, primarily because there is more precipitation along the coasts. More than half of the world's fresh water

The Transantarctic Mountains divide East Antarctica from West Antarctica. This mountain chain is 1,900 miles (3,057 km) long.

supply is inaccessible because it is locked in the ice sheets of Antarctica.

The climates of the two parts of the polar continent are quite different. Scientists who winter in the interior of the continent—the coldest spot on Earth—call the Antarctic Peninsula the "Banana Belt" because of its comparatively warmer temperatures. The Banana Belt has been known to get as warm as 48°F (9°C) in summer.

The tips of the Admiralty Mountains in Victoria Land near McMurdo Sound are all that show above thousands of feet of snow and ice.

The Great Ice Maker

The polar regions are cold for several reasons. First, the areas at the ends of the Earth receive less direct sunlight than other regions because of the planet's position in space relative to the sun. The Antarctic receives about 40 percent less sunlight than the equator in the winter.

Second, once ice began to form on the continent, the surface became so reflective that little solar energy is absorbed. Instead, it is reflected right back into space.

The third reason concerns the way the sun's energy is absorbed by land. In other regions of the Earth, the sun's energy, which arrives as short waves, is absorbed by the land and then reemitted as longer waves that are caught in the atmosphere, which in turn is warmed by them. This is the "greenhouse effect" that warms the Earth. However, in the Antarctic, the atmosphere is so clear that little long-wave radiation is caught within it.

This third reason has caused some concern among scientists about global warming. The planet's atmosphere is acquiring more and more carbon dioxide from industry and automobile exhaust. Carbon dioxide is the main gas that keeps long-wave radiation in the atmosphere. If Antarctica's atmosphere gets too warm, the ice sheet could begin to melt and raise the sea level worldwide.

All precipitation in Antarctica falls as snow. Not

much snow falls, but most of what accumulates does not melt. Loose snow piles up and is transformed into a grainy snow known as firn, or névé. As more snow falls, the firn gradually forms structured layers. Eventually, the layers are compressed, and the snow is transformed into ice "rock." Over the centuries, the "rock" gets denser until it becomes hard blue glacial ice.

Firn grains roll together and trap air between and under them. This air stays there as the snow is compressed by the weight of new snow above it, becoming glacial ice at a depth of about 200 feet (60 m). Scientists study the tiny pockets of trapped air to learn about the atmosphere on Earth through the ages.

The researchers begin by taking an ice core. A core is obtained by sending a cylinder-shaped drill down as far into the ice as possible. Back in a laboratory, the core is placed in a vacuum chamber and sliced, releasing the air that was trapped during a certain era. The air is analyzed for information, such as the amount and content of atmospheric dust and the level of carbon dioxide. For example, dust at different levels might show when major volcanic activity was occurring around the planet. Cores going back almost 200,000 years have been obtained.

Compressed layers of snow eventually become dense, blue ice.

The Moving Ice Cap

The dome of ice covering Antarctica is not a permanent, unchanging thing. Instead, the ice cap is so heavy that its own weight forces it to flow downward and outward with gravity. Toward the high center of the continent, the edges of the ice cap move perhaps only 10 to 13 feet (3 to 4 m) per year. As it gets closer to the coast of the continent, the ice moves faster—as much as 300 to 600 feet (90 to 180 m) in one year.

Two major seas lie between East and West Antarctica—the Ross and the Weddell. In these seas, as well as a few smaller areas, the moving continental ice sheet has stretched out into the water, forming ice shelves. An ice shelf is hundreds of feet thick underwater and rises up to 70 feet (21.4 m) above the water. The ice shelves stay

The Antarctic ice cap moves toward the coastline where ice breaks off into the Antarctic waters.

approximately the same thickness because, while
snow and ice are added to the top, an equal amount
of ice is taken away at the bottom by the melting
action of the warmer water beneath. In addition, ice
breaks off the outer edges of the ice shelf as huge
flat-topped, or tabular, icebergs.

In 1927, a sea captain sighted a flat-topped iceberg 100 miles (160 km) long. One of the longest-
surviving icebergs broke off about September 1967.
It had already been floating perhaps a month when
it was measured at more than 62 miles long by 30
miles wide (100 km by 50 km). It drifted for more
than two years before getting caught on rocks. Five
years later, it broke loose and traveled again. In
1976, it split in half and eventually both pieces
broke up after moving northward into ice-melting
temperatures.

The Ross Ice Shelf is about the size of Texas.
Little America, McMurdo Station, and Mount
Erebus—one of the region's two active volcanoes—
are located on this shelf. The Ross Ice Shelf was
originally called the Great Ice Barrier because a
high, vertical cliff of ice at its edge seemed insur-
mountable. Most of the expeditions to the South
Pole started on the Ross Ice Shelf or Ross Island
because, at about 800 miles (1,290 km) away, it was

the closest site to the South Pole. However, Fuchs began at the Weddell Sea on the other side of the continent and crossed by way of the South Pole to Scott Station on Ross Island. Hillary went up from Scott base, laying depots along the way, and met Fuchs at the South Pole. Scott and Shackleton left from McMurdo Sound, where there is a natural deep harbor called Winter Quarters Bay. Amundsen reached the South Pole from the western end of the Ross Ice Shelf, near Marie Byrd Land.

Glaciers

Although the ice sheet itself can be called a continental glacier, the term *glacier* is usually reserved in Antarctica for the great "rivers" of moving ice that form within the valleys of the continent. Ice builds up and forms glaciers in places where summer temperatures are too low or do not last long enough to melt the winter snow. Along the fringes of the glacier, ice ablates, or changes directly from ice into water vapor without going through a melted period first. The water begins to flow downhill when more snow ablates than falls.

Scientists don't know why glaciers move faster than the surrounding ice sheet. It may be because glaciers form over rough surfaces. As the glacier moves, the friction with the underlying surface gives off heat that melts the bottom layer of ice, lubricating the ice and helping it move. The rock below the glacier may also be warmer than the layers of ice above.

Glaciers move toward the sea where icebergs break off. The picture shows the end point of Taylor Glacier.

The fastest-known glacier lies in eastern Queen Maud Land. It travels about 1.2 miles (2 km) a year. The largest glacier in the world is Antarctica's Lambert Glacier. It is 25 miles (40 km) wide and about 250 miles (400 km) long. When it reaches the eastern edge of the continent, Lambert Glacier forms Amery Ice Shelf.

The surface of a glacier is hard and unyielding. Sometimes, when a glacier moves across a rough surface or twists around a curve, the hard surface cracks. These cracks, usually about 100 feet (30 m)

The surface of a glacier looks like hard ice, but it does not melt even on the warmest day.

deep, are called crevasses. They may be narrow enough to just step across, or 10 to 20 feet (3 to 6 m) across. Such crevasses may force travelers to find another route.

Crevasses can lead to unexpected danger and even death. Sometimes the narrow crack becomes covered with snow and traps an unwary traveler. However, some scientists willingly climb down into them, suspended by strong ropes, to take samples of ice at different levels.

Not as dangerous—but more annoying—are the phenomena called sastrugi. These occur when wind erodes the surface snow into rough, pitted shapes varying from a few inches to 6 feet (1.8 m) in height. The sastrugi harden, causing travelers great difficulty.

When a glacier reaches the coast, the glacial ice breaks off as icebergs. The process of an iceberg breaking off the glacier is called calving. Most of an iceberg—about 80 percent—lies below the surface of the water.

Icebergs come in many shapes and sizes. They are rough at first, with sharp edges, but gradually wind and heavy seas erode them into more rounded shapes. An iceberg lasts about four years before the ocean currents carry it so far north that it melts. Each year, about 5,000 icebergs break off the continental glaciers, distributing tons of fresh water throughout the salty oceans as they gradually move northward and thaw.

Exposed Land and Dry Valleys

Patches of visible land make up less than 2 percent of Antarctica. These patches don't provide water holes in the frigid desert as oases do in hot deserts. Instead, most of them are just small areas protected from blowing snow. In some places an isolated rock, called a nunatak, projects from the surrounding ice. McMurdo Station is built on an exposed area on the Ross Sea. Many exposed rocky areas serve as nurseries for penguins and other birds that breed on the continent.

The largest dry places are the dry valleys of the mountains of Victoria Land, discovered by Robert F. Scott in 1903. Though originally carved out by glaciers, the valleys are now ice-free and snow-free, and so dry that only a few lichens grow there. Geologists think dry valleys formed because the mountains rose faster than the glaciers were able to keep up with them. The valleys stay dry because

Deep cracks in glaciers are called crevasses, or chasms.

Older icebergs are sculpted by the water and wind into beautiful shapes.

the exposed rock absorbs more heat from the sun than snow does. In fact, the rock stays warm enough to melt what little snow does fall. Scientists estimate that some sections of the dry valleys have had no precipitation in the last two million years!

Two of the dry valleys contain saltwater lakes. One of them, Lake Vanda, is very deep—250 feet (75 m). The ice on its upper surface has formed in a peculiar way that transmits sunlight straight down into the water. This solar energy heats the lower levels of the water, making the bottom of this deep lake the warmest place in Antarctica. It reaches an amazing 77°F (25°C), even though a layer of ice 13 feet (4 m) thick covers the upper surface of the lake.

Fire in the Ice

The Antarctic has two active volcanoes. Mount Erebus stands 12,450 feet (3,797 m) high on the edge of McMurdo Sound and continually puffs out steam. Deception Island Volcano in the South Shetland Islands is only 1,890 feet (575 m) high. In the late 1960s, a series of volcanic eruptions on Deception Island caused such severe mud flows that British and Chilean scientists had to abandon their research bases.

Lake Vanda is a saltwater lake located in a McMurdo dry valley. The Onyx River, which only flows for a very short time on warm summer days, drains into this lake.

Scientists are studying the gases and other matter being given off by Mount Erebus in order to learn just what substances enter the Antarctic atmosphere naturally. They can then determine which elements are put into the polar atmosphere by pollution.

Green algae growing on the bottom of the ice give it a greenish hue.

Apparently, at least one other volcano is actively erupting—under the ice sheet! It was discovered in 1992 by two American scientists trying to explain the phenomenon of some glacial regions called ice streams. Ice streams flow considerably faster than the slow-moving ice on each side of them. One such ice stream is located on the downhill side of the volcano beneath the ice. Five ice streams flow from the high points of West Antarctica into the Ross Ice Shelf. The ice in one stream actually flows almost 6 feet (2 m) per day— as much as most glaciers move in a year!

Donald Blankenship, a scientist investigating the ice streams, had suggested that ice streams might have a layer of soggy sediments under them that acts like grease to allow the ice to move faster than it does in areas without such sediments. But he didn't know where the sediments got the water to keep them soggy instead of turning to rock. He had an idea that there might be places where Earth's interior heat was coming through the thin crust of bedrock. Blankenship and a colleague were testing that theory when they discovered the volcano.

Scientific instruments had revealed a large depression in the ice sheet in West Antarctica, with no obvious reason why it should be there. Blankenship and his partner were able to outline a dome-shaped volcano hidden beneath 1.25 miles (2 km) of ice. The existence of the volcano explained why ice didn't mount up in the depression. It melted instead from the bottom.

Life on the Land

Despite all the ice, there is life in the Antarctic. Most of the area's living things are found primarily in the surrounding ocean. But the continent itself also supports life.

The plants on Antarctica are mainly primitive plants such as mosses and lichens—mosslike plants that combine algae and fungi. Lichens are found within a few hundred miles of the South Pole. Some algae grow on the snow itself. These snow algae make patches of red, pink, yellow, and green on the permanent snow. Other algae form colonies on pen-

Primitive plants called lichens have adapted to the harsh Antarctic environment. There are about 350 species of lichens.

A herd of elephant seals on South Georgia Island lie in the Antarctic grass called tussock grass.

guin guano, taking nutrients from the birds' solid waste. As many as 300 species of algae grow on the continent and islands.

This land of ice and blizzards, however, is not a good place for flowers. The continent has only two species of vascular plants—more developed plants containing vessels in which fluids circulate. Most flowers, trees, and grasses are vascular plants.

One of Antarctica's vascular plants is a grass called *Deschampsia antarctica*. It grows in small clumps, especially on the islands. The other is a flowering plant called a pink or pearlwort—*Colobanthus quietensis*. Neither plant grows south of about 68° S.

A few insects and other tiny invertebrates are able to exist in the cold. However, most other living things come to the continent only temporarily, spending most of their lives in the slightly warmer sea around it.

Antarctica, which began as part of the green and tropical land of Gondwanaland, is a very different world now. Only fossils are left to tell us what kind of world it was.

Chapter Four

Life in the Cold Ocean

The treacherous doorway to Antarctica is the Drake Passage, a 600-mile (966-km) sea-lane between South America and the polar continent. Sir Francis Drake called this passage the "most mad seas." And the "maddest" seas of all come when passing through the Antarctic Convergence.

The Convergence is not just an area of rough weather. Polar scientist and writer David Campbell calls it "perhaps the longest and most important biological barrier on Earth, as formidable as any mountain range or desert." Even the color of the water changes. But more importantly, it is a critical factor in determining what living things inhabit what part of the Southern Hemisphere.

South of the Convergence, for example, there are 44 species of nesting birds, including penguins, albatrosses, petrels, skuas, and a single species each of cormorant, gull, tern, sheathbill, and pintail. That may sound like a lot, but north of the Convergence, 44 species of nesting birds can be found in a small city park.

Birds that spend all or part of their lives in the Antarctic depend on the sea for their food. However, 12 of those 44 species actually breed on the continent, depending on it for their very lives.

What Antarctica lacks in variety of species is made up for by the sheer numbers of its animals. They are fed by the nutrients the Convergence brings up from the bottom of the sea. Naturalist Ron Nuveen says, "At times there is simply too much for the human visitor to observe, too much to examine, too much with which to commune. In other words, biological overload."

The Antarctic Waters

The Antarctic waters consist of three main layers. The surface layer is approximately 330 to 500 feet (100 to 150 m) thick and not very salty because it is continually replenished by the fresh water of melting icebergs. The temperature of the water is close to freezing. Beneath the cold surface water

A gentoo penguin is distinguished by the white triangle on its forehead. Gentoos are one of 18 penguin species that breed in the Antarctic.

"The Antarctic is the south Atlantic branch of Dr. Dolittle's fantastic zoo, offering an engaging array of animals and animal assemblages."

— Ron Nuveen in Wild Ice: Antarctic Journeys

All albatrosses have tube-shaped nostrils on the upper bill. The white-capped albatross (right) nests in the Antarctic region.

lies a region of warmer water. Beneath that is the cold bottom water, which comes from the continental shelf, carrying all the chill of the ice sheet.

The ocean world on the surface is continually changing because of winds and currents. Along the coasts, the wind normally blows from east to west, like the major ocean currents. So the pack ice gradually travels in a great circle around the continent in this east wind drift. Farther away from land, the wind blows primarily from west to east, making a region called the west wind drift. Each drift area provides a different ecosystem for living things.

The outer boundary of the west wind drift is the Antarctic Convergence zone, beyond which pack ice no longer forms. Among the main inhabitants of the region are squid, which feed on crustaceans. In turn, the squid serve as food for a wide variety of animals, including sperm whales.

The east wind drift lies closer to the continent and is covered by ice much of the year. Here, the animals can eat not only the floating plankton in the sea but also algae that grow on the pack ice. Small crustaceans called krill are most abundant in the east wind drift. This food supply draws many large animals to the cold region, including at least five species of whales and six species of seals, along with numerous fish, squid, and birds.

Nature has taken on strange forms to deal with the cold temperatures. Some species, like the ice fish, have a fluid in their bodies resembling antifreeze that prevents cells from developing ice crystals. These animals have no red blood cells. Their bodies make up for the lack of oxygen with large blood vessels and a faster-beating heart. Also, these species use very little energy to maintain their body functions.

Krill—A Protein Extravaganza

The food web in the waters around Antarctica starts with phytoplankton, or tiny plants, especially the diatom class of algae, that float in the water. Like most plants, phytoplankton is capable

West Wind Drift	
East Wind Drift	Antarctic Convergence
Weddell Sea Drift	Antarctic Divergence

The map shows the direction in which the Antarctic wind drifts blow.

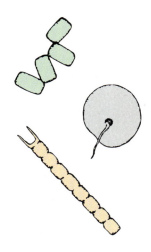

Krill eat phytoplankton, microscopic floating oceanic plants.

36

of making its own food from sunlight and carbon dioxide. Phytoplankton is eaten by zooplankton, or tiny floating animals, especially krill. Krill is a tiny shrimplike crustacean.

Krill is a Norwegian word meaning "young wriggly fish." Oddly enough, both tiny fish and the biggest animal that has ever lived—the blue whale—feed on krill. Like baleen whales, the blue whale has plates of a hard substance called baleen in its mouth instead of teeth. The blue whale sucks in huge quantities of krill along with ocean water. The krill are caught by the baleen plates and swallowed whole—up to 8,000 pounds (3,629 kg) per day per whale!

Krill are most abundant in the Weddell Sea and north and east of the Antarctic Peninsula. Squid feed on the krill, and then sperm whales and elephant seals feed on the squid. Crabeater seals, fur seals, and several penguin species also feed on krill.

Tiny crustaceans called krill are the major food source for much larger animals, such as seals and whales.

Even though krill are numbered in the billions and regularly replenished, this base of the ocean food chain may be in danger. Japan and several other countries harvest krill because it consists of about 16 percent protein, a nutrient that people need. If krill is overfished, the entire food web of Antarctica could be in danger.

Fur and Blubber

After Captain Cook reported back to England that he had seen huge numbers of seals and whales in the waters surrounding Antarctica, sealing and whaling ships converged on the Antarctic. The hunters killed millions of animals, almost destroying entire populations of fur seals, whales, and penguins.

Animals that gather in one region during a specific season are particularly vulnerable to hunting by humans. Records from the hunting season of 1820-21 show that at least 250,000 fur seals were killed with nothing more than clubs.

Polar animals are larger than their tropical relatives because of their thick layers of fur or blubber. Blubber is an insulating layer of fat that lies between the skin and muscles of cold-water animals. Humans hunted Arctic and Antarctic animals for blubber that can be boiled down into an oil that was used to light lamps and lubricate things.

Humpback whales were slaughtered during the heyday of whaling. The picture shows a humpback whale's tail flukes.

The Great Whales

Of course, the largest amount of oil came from whales. A side benefit of commercial whaling was baleen, which was used in the 1800s to stiffen corsets worn by women to achieve the fashionable "wasp" waists. The best baleen, or "whalebone," came from the southern right whale, which also produced huge amounts of oil. Whalers were thus able to obtain two different

Whaling stations, which are now abandoned (below), were established along the shores of South Georgia Island.

WHALING IN ANTARCTIC WATERS

During the heyday of whaling, the catch was measured in Blue Whale Units. For example, two and a half humpback whales, which are smaller than blue whales, were about equal to one Blue Whale Unit. Hunters, of course, preferred the blue whales because they got the most whale from a single catch. The humpback whales, about half the size of blue whales, were next in line. It only took little more than two humpbacks to equal a blue whale. They, too, were driven almost to the verge of extinction. The smaller whales required too much time and effort to catch, so they were generally left unharmed.

The other giant among the whales is the sperm whale, a toothed whale. The sperm whale eats huge quantities of squid, which it finds by diving more than 0.5 miles (0.8 km) deep in the water. The male sperm whale is about 60 feet (18 m) long, and the female is somewhat shorter. Only males venture into Antarctic waters.

Other whales that frequent the polar waters include the minke, fin, and sei—all baleen whales. The minke remained unprotected and vulnerable until 1986. The fin and sei were protected beginning in the 1970s. Of the toothed whales, only the sperm whale has ever been widely hunted. The hourglass dolphin, southern bottlenose whale, southern fourtooth whale, and the killer whale, or orca are all relatively small and have rarely been hunted.

The International Whaling Commission was established in 1946 to set limits on whaling, but it had no power to enforce its orders. Whaling continued into the 1950s, with approximately 40,000 animals killed each year. However, one by one, most nations dropped out of the hunt. By the late 1970s, only the minke remained unprotected. In 1986, an international moratorium on commercial whaling was declared. However, nations could still capture several hundred whales each year for the purpose of scientific research.

Today Japan is the world leader in whaling activity, capturing up to the maximum number of whales each year for research purposes. Norway announced in 1993 that it would also resume whaling activities. It seems that whaling, though significantly reduced, could still be a threat.

products to sell from the capture of just one whale.

Whales are free to swim in all the world's oceans, but several species are drawn south by the abundant krill supply. The blue whale, the world's largest, is an annual polar visitor. This 100-foot- (30-m-) long baleen whale spends the summer near Antarctica and migrates north for the winter months. Since a 120-ton blue whale may carry 25 tons of blubber, it is especially vulnerable to hunting. The sad reality is that there are probably only several hundred blue whales left on Earth.

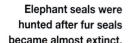

Elephant seals were hunted after fur seals became almost extinct.

Seals for Fur and Oil

The fur seals that attracted hunters to the Antarctic include the Kerguelen fur seal and the Antarctic fur seal. Their thick, velvety fur was very popular for coats and hats in the late 1700s and early 1800s.

When the populations of fur seals had been brought almost to extinction, the seal hunters began to seek out the huge, rubbery-skinned elephant seals. The elephant seal was hunted for its oil-rich blubber. Elephant seal oil was more valuable than even the best whale oil.

These animals, which may be up to 23 feet (7 m) long, don't have earflaps on the side of their heads. Above the nostrils is a mass of wrinkled flesh that the male can inflate with air, expanding it into a trunk that makes the animal's roar echo loudly.

The male elephant seal has a flap of skin that looks like an elephant's trunk when it is inflated with air.

Unlike the females of most seal species without earflaps, female elephant seals are much smaller than the males. They may be only half as long and weigh only a quarter as much. They set up nurseries on virtually all the islands of the oceans surrounding Antarctica and even up near the southern tip of South America. Each female gives birth to a single woolly pup.

The other four seal species without ear flaps in the Antarctic are the Weddell, Ross, crabeater, and leopard seals. They all live and rear their young in the pack ice region, using the sea ice within the Convergence as a place to rest and give birth. The killer whale is their major enemy. None of the four pack ice species has been much hunted by humans.

The gray body of the leopard seal is spotted around its head and along its sides. Its distinct head and longer neck make it look almost snakelike. If penguins don't keep a sharp eye out while swimming, they may be meals for this 10-foot- (3-m-) long seal. The female leopard seal is about the same size as the male, which is unusual among seals without ear flaps.

The smaller crabeater seal does not actually eat crabs. Instead, this most numerous of all seals feeds exclusively on krill. The crabeaters give birth and raise their pups on the pack ice.

The Ross seal, which is smaller yet at about 6 feet (1.8 m) long, is found only on floating ice. Ross seals dive below the pack ice to feed on squid and fish, catching them with needlelike teeth.

Perhaps the most fascinating seal is the Weddell seal. About 8 feet (2.4 m) long and weighing up to 1,000 pounds (453 kg), Weddell seals are seen by visitors more often than any other seals because they are found close to the Antarctic continent and the Antarctic bases. During the cold months, Weddell seals spend most of their time below the pack ice. They breathe through holes in the ice that they cut with their teeth. They can stay underwater for up to an hour at a time and dive as deep as 2,000 feet (600 m).

Weddell seals are primarily found on ice that is attached to solid land. A male and his harem may all use the same breathing hole, both to breathe air and to pull themselves up onto the ice. Females give

The powerful leopard seal is a dangerous predator of penguins.

The Weddell seal does not migrate. It spends winters under the ice, using its teeth to gnaw air holes. This seal is well known for its diving prowess.

birth on these anchored ice areas in the early austral spring (October).

Penguins, Charmers of the Ice

Penguins would not have survived through the ages if there had been predators on their icy world. But modern times and human predators almost finished them off.

When the hunters failed to bring in a big catch of seals or whales, they often went after penguins. These charming birds also have a thick layer of fat under their skin. Penguins were killed, and their fat was boiled down to provide oil to lubricate the great machines of the industrial nations. One penguin produced about a pint (0.47 l) of oil. The slaughter continued until the penguin populations had been reduced below the level where it was practical to keep killing them. Since that time, penguin populations have mostly replenished themselves.

Penguins probably would not have survived at all if their meat tasted better. Dr. Frederick Cook, a polar explorer, described penguin meat as "a piece of beef, odorous cod fish and a canvas-backed duck roasted together in a pot, with blood and cod-liver oil for sauce."

Today, 21 species of penguins breed on various

Penguins are perfectly adapted to the cold climate of Antarctica. Often it is hard to see them against the white snow.

islands throughout the Southern Hemisphere. All penguins are primarily black and white, which makes them difficult to see from either above or below when they are in water. Their feathers overlap, locking together to keep water out. Under the outer feathers, a layer of down next to the skin keeps out the cold. Also, like cold-water mammals, penguins have a thick layer of blubber for insulation.

Emperor penguin adults vomit partially digested food from their own stomachs to feed their young.

Instead of swimming, penguins literally glide through the water. Their short flippers work like propellers, and their webbed feet and short tails all function together like a rudder. They have the speed and the ability to dive after fast fish, though some feed mostly on the more easily captured krill.

Only the Adélie and emperor penguins actually breed on the Antarctic continent. The Adélie requires some dry land for laying its egg and raising its chick. Then the bird moves onto the pack ice for the winter, where the temperatures are warmer than on land.

The emperor isn't so lucky. It has to set up its nursery on ice. The largest of all penguins, the emperor penguin's breeding cycle is too long to fit into the short Antarctic summer. This 3-foot- (1-m-) tall bird has had to develop behaviors that compensate for the cold. The female lays her egg in June—the middle of the polar winter. Then she abandons her mate and her egg for a season of fishing in the ocean. The male, who goes without food for eight or nine weeks, finds a comfortable spot to stand in an area protected from the wind by sea cliffs or icebergs. There he maneuvers the egg up onto the tops of his feet. A warm, cozy flap of skin on his abdomen covers the egg, keeping it warm.

It would be impossible for one male standing alone to keep an egg warm enough to incubate it. But thousands of emperor penguins—sometimes as many as 6,000—huddle together on the ice. Birds on the outer edges of the huddle continually struggle

The best-known penguin species is the Adélie penguin. Here an Adélie penguin sits on a nest made from pebbles stolen from neighbors.

Penguins look very clumsy walking on land, but they are accomplished swimmers in the water.

toward the inside of the group, while those already inside try to keep their warm locations.

The male spends about 60 days incubating the egg. When the downy brown chick hatches, the mother returns from the sea, and the starved father, who has lost up to half of his total weight, heads for the ocean and food. The female then rears the chick, which must be protected from marauding sea birds as well as the bitter cold for at least six weeks, until it can fend for itself.

Smaller penguins, such as the Adélie, gentoo, and chinstrap, are all about 18 inches (46 cm) tall—just about the right size to make a good meal for leopard seals. Since penguins have no way to fight, they usually make a spectacular escape. They swim as rapidly as possible to gather momentum, and then they leap vertically out of the water onto the pack ice.

The gentoo has a triangle-shaped white patch on its forehead. The chinstrap has a black marking that looks like a chinstrap stretching around its face beneath the beak. The gentoo and chinstrap nest primarily on islands within the Antarctic Convergence.

Nesting on the islands outside the Convergence are the king, macaroni, and rockhopper penguins. The smallest is the little rockhopper, which has yellow feathers sticking out from its head and a somewhat belligerent look on its face. The macaroni, which has orange plumes on its head, is named for

A chinstrap penguin is distinguished by the small black marking beneath its eyes and beak resembling the strap of a hat.

Macaroni penguins have distinctive orange plumes on their heads.

the "Yankee Doodle Dandy" line that contains "stuck a feather in his cap."

The king penguin is about the size of the emperor penguin, but it has more vivid orange patches on its head and a gold-to-orange coloring around the throat. Like the emperor, it has a thick layer of fat and was consequently hunted almost to extinction. Also like the emperor, king penguins lay only one egg at a time, although both parents help to incubate the egg. It takes more than a year to raise the single chick.

Over the Sea

While leopard seals threaten penguins in the water, the biggest danger to penguins on land comes from other birds. The main predators are skuas, the scavengers of the Antarctic. These birds, related to gulls, eat primarily fish and krill but will take advantage of any absentmindedness on the part of a penguin parent in order to grab an egg or baby bird.

Skuas spend most of their time at sea, often traveling as far north as Japan. However, the McCormick's skua nests on the Antarctic continent, building little roosting places of pebbles and moss on the gravel. The brown skua nests primarily on islands outside the Convergence, although some can be found inside the Convergence at Palmer Station.

Also a danger to penguin hatchlings are pigeonlike birds called sheathbills. These birds eat anything, living or dead, and even congregate over the body of a dead seal.

Albatrosses, which often spend the summer in the Antarctic, belong to an order of birds called petrels. Petrels are birds with long tube-shaped nostrils on top of their beaks. The nostrils have special glands that remove salt from the bird's body. Giant petrels have the strange ability to vomit the contents of their stomach forcibly over several feet

A black-browed albatross searches for food over the Antarctic sea.

A wandering albatross spreads is wings next to a giant petrel. The tubes on top of the petrel's beak are used to expel salt water. A petrel chick (right) looks nothing like its parent.

in order to scare away intruders in their area.

Black-and-white-speckled cape pigeons, also a type of petrel, follow ships for whatever garbage they can pick up. The cape pigeon population exploded during the whaling era thanks to all the whale waste the ships left behind. The numbers returned to normal when the whaling industry slowed.

Besides penguins, two other land birds live within the Antarctic Convergence the year round. One is a duck called the yellow-billed pintail, and the other is the South Georgia pipit, the only Antarctic songbird.

The most amazing bird that spends time in the Antarctic is the Arctic tern. Perhaps this bird can't get enough polar weather. It raises its young in the north polar region during the Arctic summer, and lives in the pack ice region during the Antarctic summer. To accomplish this, the Arctic tern makes an annual journey of 25,000 miles (40,000 km), flying day and night for almost nine months. A very similar Antarctic tern stays home in the south, raising its young on the continent and most islands. It spends the winter at sea, probably on pack ice.

Much is still not known about the Antarctic animals. The vast expanses of ice and ocean hide many secrets that human visitors have not yet been able to discover.

Chapter Five

A Continent for Science

The first century of exploration in Antarctica was a combination of voyages of discovery and observation by numerous people with scientific curiosity. It was an unexplored continent, open to anyone who could fund an expedition or to any member of a sealing or whaling expedition who happened to write down what he saw.

True international cooperation began in 1875 when German explorer Lt. Karl Weyprecht of the Austro-Hungarian Navy proposed that several countries cooperate in taking measurements at both poles at the same time. The result, the First International Polar Year (1882-83), saw ten countries establishing stations in the Arctic and three in the Antarctic. The data collected at these stations produced the most accurate map of our planet's magnetic field made up to that time.

In 1895, when the Sixth International Geographic Congress on Antarctica met, the nations agreed that it was time to start exploring that icy world again. They drew routes to be used in exploring the continent so that work wouldn't be duplicated.

In 1897, the first major scientific expedition took place under the leadership of Belgian naval officer Adrien Victor Joseph de Gerlache. The scientists on the expedition made useful observations of stars, weather, ocean currents, and ice dimensions.

The era of heroic exploration was directed primarily toward reaching the South Pole, and science appeared to have been put temporarily on the back burner in favor of the competition. However, science was a major interest of Robert F. Scott's. One of the factors contributing to the death of his polar group was Scott's reluctance to let them stop pulling the sled containing rock samples.

American naval officer Richard E. Byrd and pilot Bernt Balchen startled the world in 1929 by making a flight to and from the South Pole, the first people to do so. However, Byrd sought more information about the weather in Antarctica and returned to his base at Little America in 1934. He took with him a large party of scientists. One group

Antarctica "stands as a challenge to man's fortitude and to his ingenuity, not only in finding ways to cope with its severe climate . . . but also in devising political institutions that will keep it what it has—perhaps only temporarily— become: a highly successful experiment in international cooperation."

— Walter Sullivan in Frozen Future: A Prophetic Report from Antarctica, 1973

In a nationwide contest in 1928, an American Boy Scout was chosen to accompany Richard E. Byrd to Antarctica. The winner was 19-year-old Paul Siple, a native of Montpelier, Ohio. Almost thirty years later, Siple, who fell in love with the southern polar region on his first journey, became the scientific leader of the permanent station established by the United States at the South Pole during the International Geophysical Year.

FLIGHT TO THE POLE

Today, flights to the South Pole are fairly routine, but in 1929, when Richard E. Byrd and pilot Bernt Balchen made their flight, it was a fearful adventure. There was no radio and no landmarks by which to navigate. Compasses were not accurate that close to the South magnetic pole. And their airplane—a Ford Tri-motor—was unable to climb high enough to get over the Transantarctic Mountains on the route from Little America at the Bay of Whales to the South Pole. They had to fly through a very narrow pass created by a glacier.

The plane carried four men as it took off on November 29, 1929. When they reached the pass through the mountains, they had to dump either fuel or food—and either decision might be fatal. They chose to jettison food, and, pound by pound, the plane lightened enough to clear the mountains.

Then they depended completely on Byrd as navigator to get them across hundreds of miles of bleak, featureless ice cap to the South Pole and take them back to a storage area where fuel had been placed earlier. They arrived back at Little America, having completed the trip in 15 hours and 51 minutes—a journey that had taken Roald Amundsen about 12 weeks.

The Byrd Monument (left) is located at McMurdo scientific station.

succeeded in measuring the depth of the ice cap.

Byrd spent the winter alone in a tiny station on the Ross Ice Shelf. Each day, he radioed weather data back to Little America. After almost dying of carbon monoxide poisoning from a faulty heater, he wrote, "That night, as never before, I discovered how alone I was."

The Second Polar Year, held during 1932-33, had 44 nations participating. Unfortunately, World War II interfered with the publication of the data.

Research Bases

In 1939, the United States created the U.S. Antarctic Service. Its initial work was under the leadership of Admiral Byrd. For the first time, the government had taken charge of American involvement in polar science.

Byrd established the first permanent American research base, East Base, on Stonington Island near the end of the Antarctic Peninsula. A new expedition returned in 1947-48 to complete the mapping of that little-known coastline.

After World War II, the United States held the largest polar expedition ever. Called Operation High-Jump, it was a military exercise involving almost 5,000 men. Its object was to give the troops polar experience in the event of a showdown with the Soviet Union. However, instead of war, an era of cooperation in the name of science was about to start with the International Geophysical Year (IGY).

There were five Little America stations. The first two supported Byrd expeditions in 1928–30 and 1933–35. The last one, Little America V (above), was an IGY station that operated between 1955 and 1959. Part of its walls were caught up in an iceberg that calved from the Ross Ice Shelf in 1987.

McMurdo Station is America's largest Antarctic base. Built on volcanic rock, it spreads along the shore of Ross Island.

In preparation for the IGY, the United States carried out Operation Deepfreeze from 1955 to 1957. The aim was to set up a major base on McMurdo Sound as the launching site for moving materials around the continent. Several bases were erected, but the most complicated task was building the Amundsen-Scott station at the South Pole. All the construction material had to be flown in, along with everything else needed by the people who would winter there.

The largest research station, McMurdo Station on Ross Island, is operated by the United States. McMurdo Station was started in 1955 with a few tents as a staging base for people going inland to work. Today it is a whole town, growing out of the rocky surface of the island. Its sea-ice runway and year-round runway on a nearby glacier are used by most scientists arriving on the continent. From there they spread out to other bases, usually traveling by helicopter and airplanes. The glacier does not move quickly enough to disrupt the runway. The town is sheltered from the katabatic winds by high ground.

There are more than a thousand scientists and support personnel—both men and women—living at McMurdo Station during the summer. Both the site and the work are supported by the Office of Polar Programs of the National Science Foundation.

The British base of Rothera on the southern Antarctic Peninsula is smaller than McMurdo

The U.S. Amundsen-Scott base at the South Pole was built on the ice in 1957, as part of the IGY, but it was later covered with new snow and ice, which turned it into an underground—or under-ice—station. Gradually crushed by the ice, the original station was replaced in the 1970s by new buildings sheltered under a protective dome. To date, the new protective dome has not been damaged by snow and ice.

Station and probably more typical. It has several wooden buildings, including a two-story dwelling for 40 or 50 people who work there during the summer. About a dozen people remain in the winter, carrying on the earth-science research that is their prime reason for being in Antarctica.

The area with the largest number of bases is King George Island, with bases for seven different countries and 300 workers. The most remote base is Russia's Vostok Base, located on top of the continental ice cap at the farthest point from all coasts.

Living on "The Ice"

The work of a biologist, geologist, glaciologist, meteorologist, or oceanographer requires a great deal of concentration. And how much more complicated that work can be when it is done during a blizzard or in bitter cold surrounded by glaring ice!

This ecologist is studying a rock sample. Scientists working in the cold, harsh Antarctic environment must dress in layers of warm clothing and protect their eyes from the sun.

Researchers who stay out on "The Ice" for more than a few hours must wear numerous layers of clothing to protect against the bitter cold and the wind. Insulated mittens and boots are crucial. Goggles help to protect the eyes from the wind and glare. There's no running quickly between buildings without adequate protection. Even the slightest errand must be planned and dressed for.

Everything the researchers eat has to be brought to the continent, except the food grown in greenhouses at some bases. The people also need a great deal of water to drink. The water from the ocean has to have the salt removed for drinking, or else ice can be melted.

Working through the winter is not easy. The United States has three research stations that function the year round. Potential workers must pass stringent psychological tests to be sure they can withstand the stress of isolation and boredom. People who spend five months in almost perpetual darkness at close quarters with each other—and with no privacy—have to be specially selected for their psychological strength. Some people staying

Food and plants are grown in the greenhouse at McMurdo.

any length of time develop a condition called "big eye," in which they occasionally go into a trance-like state.

One situation that can bring on mental confusion is whiteout. This occurs when everything on the ground is uniformly white, and the sky is filled with white stratus clouds. The white sky and the white ice reflect each other, making orientation impossible. A person walking outdoors has no depth perception, which can bring on nausea and panic. Occasionally, a whiteout may last for several days.

But whatever the difficulties, most scientists feel that a season or two on The Ice is a privilege. Many want to return again and again.

Argentina has several small bases on Antarctica. Almirante Brown is located on the Antarctic Peninsula near America's Palmer scientific station.

Dividing up a Continent

During the initial years of Antarctic exploration, other expeditions investigated the fringes of the continent. And based on those investigations, various countries claimed parts of Antarctica. Many of the claims overlapped, while other parts of the continent were not claimed at all. Everything from establishing a base to providing mail service—even having a head of state visit—served as reason enough for a region to belong to a specific country.

At the end of the exploration period, Great Britain, France, Australia, Norway, New Zealand, Chile, and Argentina all claimed specific regions. However, two major countries were not involved in these claims at all. The United States, though it had the basis for various claims, never made a claim and never recognized the others. The U.S. government stated that a claim is not valid unless followed by effective occupation. The Soviet Union refused to recognize any other country's claim, but claimed the whole continent for itself on the basis of the Bellingshausen expedition.

Antarctica is set aside for scientific research. Scientists study ice cores to learn more about former climates and earlier atmospheric conditions.

International Geophysical Year

Over many decades, nations argued about their claims to various pieces of the polar region, but nothing was decided. While the politicians argued, the scientists took things into their own hands.

Until about 1950, geophysicists—researchers studying the Earth—worked primarily alone. One

Helicopters deliver equipment to scientists at tent camps erected for field studies during the summer months.

person would take measurements—either at one place over time, or at one time over several places. Then some researchers, led by Dr. Lloyd Berkner, suggested that by developing international cooperation—which had a history of working in Antarctica—research into the whole Earth could be coordinated and more meaningful. The International Geophysical Year (IGY) was born.

Among the main objectives of the IGY was the study of the upper atmosphere and worldwide meteorology. Two main focuses of investigation involved space and Antarctica, making the IGY, in effect, the Third Polar Year. The time chosen was July 1, 1957, to December 31, 1958, to coincide with the maximum activity of the sun. With measurements being taken all over the Earth, scientists could reach a clearer understanding of the influence of the sun.

Twelve nations established 40 research stations on Antarctica, plus 20 more on various islands, including one at the South Pole by the Americans and one, Vostok Base, at the geographic pole by the Russians. The British Commonwealth nations cooperated on Fuchs's Trans-Antarctic Expedition.

While a great deal of data were obtained during the IGY, two events stood out. The first artificial satellite to successfully orbit the Earth was launched by the Soviet Union on October 4, 1957. Its success initiated a space race with the United States that continued for several decades. The other major development was the Antarctic Treaty, which spurred the move to preserve the polar region for science.

Scientists launch balloons to study conditions of the upper atmosphere.

The Antarctic Treaty

The International Geophysical Year put nations that normally argued with each other in a cooperative mood. The United States sent a letter to the other participating nations proposing that they draw up a treaty setting aside the entire continent for scientific research.

The result of their discussions was the Antarctic Treaty. It was signed on December 1, 1959, by Argentina, Australia, Belgium, Chile, France, Japan, New Zealand, Norway, the Union of South Africa, the Soviet Union, the United Kingdom, and the United States of America.

By setting aside the issue of ownership of Antarctica, the treaty made it a continent for science. In the years following the original signing, several other nations became major partners in the agreement, including Germany, China, Uruguay, India, Brazil, Italy, and Poland.

Because the treaty was created during the Cold War, one of its most important provisions was to keep Antarctica free of nuclear testing. Each nation recognized—in the words of the treaty—"that it is in the interest of all mankind that Antarctica shall continue forever to be used exclusively for peaceful purposes and shall not become the scene or object of international discord."

The treaty has paid off in many ways. David Sugden, in *Arctic and Antarctic*, wrote: "The benefits flowing from the Antarctic Treaty are immense. In place of the slide into political and even military rivalry which seemed only too likely in the early 1950s, the Antarctic Treaty has substituted an atmosphere of peace and cooperation."

The claims have not been forgotten, but they have, by international agreement, been set aside for a greater, scientific good. How long the situation will last depends on developments in the future.

Biologists study the animal species of Antarctica during the warmer summer months.

The U.S. station of McMurdo and the Russian station of Molodezhnaya (shown below) are the largest bases on Antarctica.

An icebreaker makes its way toward Antarctica through frozen seas. As more people come to Antarctica to visit or to study, environmental problems are created in this fragile ecosystem.

Chapter Six

Saving a Continent

Until a few decades ago, only one or two human beings at a time had ever set foot in the Antarctic. But the signs that humans have been there are unmistakable. Fires have broken out in garbage dumps, and nothing is cleaned up. Body waste lies on the ice and never deteriorates. Vehicles are left where they break down or dragged onto the pack ice to sink when the ice melts. Items that cost a lot to take home are simply abandoned.

The nations that signed the Antarctic Treaty knew that the environment was going to require special consideration. In 1964, they developed a program called Agreed Measures for the Conservation of Antarctic Fauna and Flora, which made everything south of 60° S "a special conservation area." That agreement has, to some extent, protected the wildlife, but it's becoming clear that the air, land, and water must also be protected.

Air Pollution

In 1987, D. W. H. Walton wrote in *Antarctic Science,* "It would be a grave mistake for the world

53

to ignore the contribution which Antarctic science can make towards solving or warning about global problems. All mankind...needs to be aware of the potential for future catastrophe residing in major global problems...." Antarctica is currently playing a role in at least two atmospheric environmental concerns—the ozone layer and global warming.

For many years people paid little attention to the idea that laboratory-made chemicals called chlorofluorocarbons (CFCs) might be harming the upper atmosphere. These chemicals were designed not to react with other chemicals and were widely used in aerosol spray cans and industrial cleaning processes. There was no proof that the chemicals rose to the upper atmosphere, where, in the presence of sunlight, the chlorine in the molecule had the power to break molecules of ozone in the upper atmosphere (O_3) into regular oxygen (O_2). The layer of ozone is vitally important because it stops harmful ultraviolet rays in sunlight from entering our atmosphere.

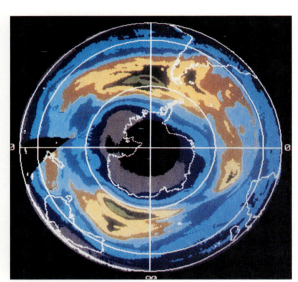

The Antarctic ozone "hole" is the oval feature generally covering the Antarctic, portrayed in gray and violet colors. This picture was produced from data gathered by a satellite that monitors the ozone over the entire Earth every day.

Then in the early 1980s, Joe Farman, a scientist with the British Antarctic Survey at Faraday Station, discovered an area over the Antarctic where the ozone layer was much thinner than elsewhere. He called it a "hole" in the ozone. Over several years, his measurements revealed that the size of the hole fluctuates with the seasons, but that it is apparently always getting bigger. As the hole grows in size, people living in exposed areas have an increasing risk of developing skin cancer due to overexposure to ultraviolet rays. Exposed areas include much of Australia and the southern tips of South America and Africa.

Global warming refers to the possibility that the base temperature of Earth's atmosphere is rising. Many scientists believe that this is occurring primarily because automobiles and industry have added too much carbon dioxide (CO_2) and other gases to the atmosphere. These gases add to the heat-trapping ability of the atmosphere.

Antarctica may act as a research center for the whole question of global warming. The ice cores removed from glaciers show clearly that at times

A NASA scientist reviews data for an ozone mapping experiment. This experiment uses laser beams to determine the extent of ozone above a flying laboratory.

when there was more CO_2 in the atmosphere, the temperature was warming, and there was more melting. They don't show, however, which came first—the temperature change or the carbon dioxide. Nor do they show if it is happening now. Too many unknowns are involved at present to reach firm conclusions.

Antarctica might also be a victim of global warming. As the planet's temperature rises, the surface ice melts. If too much fresh water enters the sea, the natural balance of the water surrounding Antarctica might change.

If all the ice in Antarctica melted, the oceans would rise worldwide about 265 feet (80 m), submerging major parts of every continent. But even if the planet is getting warmer because of excess carbon dioxide and other gases in the atmosphere, the Antarctic ice is not going to melt anytime soon. However, there could be enough heat buildup in the next 200 or 300 years to melt the West Antarctic ice sheet enough to make it slide into the ocean. That alone would flood Florida, parts of England, and many other low-lying regions.

Debris left to rust is a big problem in Antarctica (left). A seal pup finds shelter in some rusting equipment (above).

The Problem of Waste

Waste disposal is the biggest continuing problem in Antarctica. Every human being who goes to the frigid continent generates 4.4 pounds (2 kg) of waste each day, and the low temperatures prevent materials of any kind from decomposing. At Scott's shack at Cape Evans on Ross Island, the broken body of a sled dog still lies where it fell in 1911.

For decades, especially around McMurdo Station, waste was allowed to accumulate in pits, where it was periodically burned. That practice was stopped in 1991. Then attempts were made to burn the materials in an incinerator, or special burning chamber. Burning waste in incinerators still releases chemicals that could poison ice and water. Although that was acceptable under the Antarctic Treaty, environmental groups persuaded U.S. courts that the U.S. bases must conform to Environmental Protection Agency standards.

McMurdo was rebuilt in the 1980s to make it environmentally sound. A new landfill was constructed. Equipment and buildings were rebuilt to use less energy. The "town" was moved onto a series of level terraces, and all waste was removed by U.S. ships. The waste was then disposed of according to the standards of the U.S. Environmental Protection Agency.

Waste used to lie in dumps at McMurdo Station. Since the 1980s however, this practice has stopped.

The Need for Energy

In 1961, the U.S. Navy installed a nuclear energy reactor on a hill next to McMurdo Station to provide "clean" energy for the station. They proudly announced the opening of the "first and only nuclear power plant on the Antarctic continent." The reactor provided power and fresh water to McMurdo Station for many years.

Unfortunately, the reactor suffered from a radiation leak and was temporarily shut down in 1972. The navy decided that repairing it would be too expensive. Tearing the plant down turned out to be slightly more difficult than building it. Several tons of radioactive earth and rock had to be removed and taken to the United States by ship before the site was decontaminated.

Tourists to the Great Southland

Tourists started going to the Antarctic in 1956. Cruise ships and private yachts now dock at the Antarctic Peninsula, especially near Palmer Station, and airplanes fly in from "nearby" land. Without air-traffic control or navigational aids, the possibility of tourist-related accidents increases.

In 1979, an Air New Zealand tourist flight over Antarctica crashed into the side of Mount Erebus. All 257 people aboard were killed. As a result, the National Science Foundation decided to have nothing to do with privately arranged visits to the polar region. The crash stopped airline flights over the South Pole, but it certainly did not stop tourism. Today, people are even flying in from South America to ski on the mountains of the Antarctic Peninsula.

In 1989, an Argentinean supply ship carrying about 90 tourists as well as supplies for the Argentine base ran aground on a rocky shoal near Palmer Station. Approximately 250,000 gallons (946,350 l) of diesel fuel flooded into the waters. Among other damage, the fuel wiped out a colony of skua chicks. This focused the world's attention on what was beginning to happen in Antarctica.

Some people would like to create tourist facilities in Antarctica for people who love adventure and winter sports. However, increased human activity on the continent could lead to complex problems and damage to the environment. Waste disposal, public safety, and local governmental authority could become problematic issues.

Tourist visits may lead to more oil spills and damage to fragile habitats. In addition, accidents interfere with scientific research, which must be tightly scheduled in the region's limited summer months.

In January 1993, a ranger from the United States National Park Service went to Palmer Station to brief tourists on what they would see and what they should and should not do to protect the area. The park service did not know if it would permanently station a ranger in Antarctica during the polar summers, but it seems unlikely that tourists will stop coming.

A New Age

No one knows for certain what natural resources might lie under the ice. Various minerals such as coal and copper have been found, but all governments have agreed that the costs of getting the ore out of the ground and transporting it back to civilization are just too great.

The biggest threat to Antarctica is the need for new sources of minerals. Luckily, at present, there

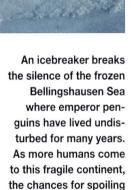

An icebreaker breaks the silence of the frozen Bellingshausen Sea where emperor penguins have lived undisturbed for many years. As more humans come to this fragile continent, the chances for spoiling animal habitat increase.

These tourists near the Weddell Sea are busy taking pictures of a penguin.

is little interest in the coal and iron ore located in the mountains. The most attractive potential resource is oil, and there are probably large reserves under the Ross, Bellingshausen, and Weddell seas.

In 1988, the parties to the Antarctic Treaty signed the Convention for the Regulation of Antarctic Mineral Resource Activities (CRAMRA). It called for agreement of all the parties before any mining could take place. But environmental groups thought that the very existence of such an agreement implied that mining might be acceptable at some time. They wanted a new agreement calling for a complete and permanent ban on mineral exploration. France and Australia took the lead in fighting for such a ban by refusing to sign CRAMRA in 1989.

Congressman Wayne Owens of Utah said in congressional hearings in 1990, "We do not need Antarctica's minerals. But we do need a pristine Antarctica. We need it for baseline measures of alarming global trends toward global warming and ozone depletion. We need it for its undisturbed ecosystem which helps to feed the world. We are not that desperately poor to risk this precious ecosystem for a few days or months of oil."

The Protocol on Environmental Protection to the Antarctic Treaty was signed in 1991 and ratified by the U.S. Senate in October 1992. Among other things, it placed an indefinite ban on exploitation of mineral resources in the Antarctic. It also called for a 50-year ban on both mining of and exploration for mineral resources. After that, mining might be possible with consent of two-thirds of the signers.

Richard Laws, former director of the British Antarctic Survey, thinks that no agreement is likely to have a lasting effect. "If Antarctic minerals should in future become essential to the world—despite their enormous cost—then whatever action is taken now to ban mining, a consensus will be found to reverse it."

People have jokingly talked about towing icebergs north someday to give people fresh, unpolluted water. However, when groundwater runs out in such places as the Middle East—as it

Antarctica has many mineral resources. Lava, iron (the reddish material), and ice can be seen compressed together in the picture above.

Some people are looking at icebergs as a resource for fresh water as water supplies diminish over the Earth.

could within 40 or 50 years—it may not be so funny. Antarctica may indeed be mined for its water! But that resource will be lost if the glaciers and the ocean they feed into become polluted.

The World Park

The idea of a world park was first proposed in 1972 by New Zealand. A world park would be like a national park but would have support from all nations. However, New Zealand was the only country interested at that time because most nations were not ready to give up their individual specific claims.

Greenpeace set up World Park, the only nongovernment base in Antarctica.

Greenpeace, an international environmental organization, later brought up the idea again. They said that a world park would be based on four principles: protection of wilderness values; protection of all wildlife, though limited fishing would be allowed; cooperation among scientists for limited scientific activity; and freedom from all weapons.

Greenpeace workers soon realized that people in the organization would have to actually go to Antarctica if they wanted to be heard. In 1987, Greenpeace environmentalists established the only nongovernment base in Antarctica, called World Park. They hoped their base would qualify them to be an official observer at Antarctic Treaty meetings. Greenpeace drew the attention of the world—with alarming photographs—to some of the practices at McMurdo Station. The environmentalists successfully stopped the construction of an airfield at Dumont D'Urville, the French base. And after inspecting a number of bases, they called attention to toxic-waste disposal dumps that might be affecting wildlife. The increased media exposure led to the clean-up of these disposal sites.

By 1994, Greenpeace decided they would soon need to dismantle the base and use their funds to fight for the World Park idea in other ways. They promised that in removing their base, Greenpeace would leave no trace on the pristine ice world that they had ever been there.

It's Not Too Late

The environments of all other continents have been permanently affected by the careless behavior of humans. Many of the plant and animal species that inhabit them may never again thrive in the wild. But it's not too late for Antarctica. It can still be a land completely devoted to peace and science.

American naturalist Henry David Thoreau wrote that a person is rich in proportion to the number of things he can afford to leave alone. We have plundered the riches of the rest of the Earth. Let's think about the incredible icy world of Antarctica—and let's leave it alone.

The Antarctic sky at midnight near Palmer Station is breathtakingly beautiful.

GLOSSARY

Convergence – the path around the continent of Antarctica where cold polar waters meet and move under warmer water coming from the north. Weather patterns change at the Antarctic Convergence, and many animals are drawn to the living things that rise from the bottom of the sea.

crevasse – a deep crack in a glacier, which may be covered with snow and hidden, making it dangerous to travelers; also called a chasm.

dead reckoning – a method of navigation that requires keeping careful track of distances traveled and turns made.

glacial – occurring in or on a glacier, or having the temperature of a glacier.

glaciation – the formation of glaciers on land or water.

glacier – a "river" of ice that has compacted with time and that flows under the force of its own weight from a higher elevation to a lower one.

global warming – the concept that the Earth's atmosphere is gradually getting warmer because of the increasing amount of carbon dioxide and other molecules put into it by people burning fossil fuels, such as coal, oil, and natural gas.

greenhouse effect – the normal warmth of Earth's atmosphere caused by the tendency of carbon dioxide and certain other molecules to absorb and reflect the heat radiation from the sun back toward the planet instead of out into space.

katabatic – downward flowing. Katabatic winds are winds that are driven by the force of gravity, moving masses of very cold air rapidly downward from the peak of the Antarctic continent to the coasts. They may reach 200 miles per hour (321 kph).

latitude – a position on the Earth's surface parallel to the equator, which is at 0° latitude. The South Pole is located at 90° South latitude.

magnetic pole – the point toward which a compass is drawn; unlike the geographic pole, it moves because the liquid iron core of the Earth moves. The South magnetic pole is many miles from the geographic South Pole.

nunatak – an isolated rock sticking out of surrounding ice and snow.

sastrugi – snow blown into rough, jagged peaks that harden, causing danger to travelers.

scurvy – a disease caused by lack of vitamin C in the diet, characterized by easy bruising, loss of teeth, and eventual death.

sextant – an instrument used to measure the angle between a known star and the Earth's horizon. The angle is then checked against a published listing that shows star angles on various dates. The result is the latitude at which the ship or traveler is located. Sextants are used in celestial, or star, navigation.

Also see "An Ice Glossary" on page 12.

FOR MORE INFORMATION

Books

Antarctica: Great Stories from the Frozen Continent. Sydney, Australia: Reader's Digest Pty. Ltd., 1985.

Byrd, Richard E. *Alone*. New York: Putnam, 1938.

Campbell, David G. *The Crystal Desert: Summers in Antarctica*. Boston: Houghton Mifflin, 1992.

Hackwell, W. John. *Desert of Ice: Life and Work in Antarctica*. New York: Scribner, 1991.

James, Barbara. *Conserving Our World: Conserving the Polar Regions*. Austin, Tex.: Steck-Vaughn, 1991.

Lord, Barbara. *The New Explorers: Women in Antarctica*. NY: Dodd, Mead & Co., 1981.

Neider, Charles, editor. *Antarctica: Authentic Accounts of Life and Exploration in the World's Highest, Driest, Windiest, Coldest and Most Remote Continent*. New York: Random House, 1972.

Nuveen, Ron, Colin Monteath, Tui De Roy, and Mark Jones. *Wild Ice: Antarctic Journeys.* Washington and London: Smithsonian Institution Press, 1990.

Pyne, Stephen J. *The Ice: A Journey to Antarctica.* Iowa City: University of Iowa Press, 1986.

Sandal, Cass R. *The Arctic and Antarctic.* New Frontiers: Exploration in the 20th Century series. NY: Franklin Watts, 1987.

Seth, Ronald. *Let's Visit Antarctica.* London: Burke, 1983.

Sipiera, Paul P. *Roald Amundsen and Robert Scott.* The World's Great Explorers series. Chicago: Childrens Press, 1990.

Steward, Gail B. *Antarctica.* Places in the News series. NY: Crestwood House, 1991.

Swan, Robert. *Destination: Antarctica.* NY: Scholastic, Inc., 1988.

Walton, D.W.H., editor. *Antarctic Science,* Cambridge: Cambridge University Press, 1987.

Winckler, Suzanne, and Mary M. Rodgers. *Antarctica.* Our Endangered Planet series. Minneapolis: Lerner Publications Co., 1992.

Videos

Exploring Antarctica. Finley Holiday Film Corp.

Mutual of Omaha's Spirit of Adventure. *Antarctic Odyssey.* MPI Home Video.

Search for Adventure. *Antarctic Challenge.*

The Cousteau Collection, Vol. 2. *Lilliput in Antarctica.*

INDEX